Living in the Supernatural

Kathie Walters

Published by

GOOD NEWS FELLOWSHIP MINISTRIES
220 Sleepy Creek Rd..
Macon, GA 31210
Phone:(912)757-8071 Fax:(912)757-0136

Published by

GOOD NEWS FELLOWSHIP MINISTRIES
220 Sleepy Creek Rd.
Macon, GA 31210
Phone:(912)757-8071   Fax:(912)757-0136

Printed by : FAITH PRINTING
4210 Locust Hill Road
Taylors, S.C. 29687

This book is dedicated first of all to the lovely Holy Spirit. It is really all about Him. Its purpose is to encourage you, the reader, to honor and treasure His presence, for His awesome and wonderful ways are glorious.

Second, it is dedicated to my precious sisters in the Lord who let me see more of Jesus through them. I love them because they hunger for an intimate relationship with the Holy Spirit, who reveals Jesus.

Third, I dedicate this book to my friend Joy Strang, who motivated me to write what was in my heart although it seemed an enormous undertaking. Thank you, Joy. You are a great encourager.

Much appreciation goes to my very patient husband, David, and my beautiful daughters, Faith and Lisa-Joy. They are a joy and a delight.

CONTENTS

INTRODUCTION

When we are born again, we are delivered from the power of darkness and translated into the kingdom of God's dear Son (Col. 1:13). By this we begin to live in a supernatural realm. Life in this realm is more than reading a Bible, attending church and trying to live morally. The Christian life in its essence is being filled with the Spirit (Eph. 5:18), living in the Spirit and walking in the Spirit (Gal. 5:25). Many Christians have never experienced this on a day-to-day basis.

Kathie shares scores of insights and personal experiences, including my experiences and those of others, which will help you see that the Spirit-filled life is God's norm for His children. Each chapter reveals a number of keys to making your Christian life an ongoing exciting adventure.

David Walters

ONE

A NEW BEGINNING

B efore being filled with the Holy Spirit, I had a great deal of head knowledge. Martyn Lloyd-Jones of Westminster Chapel, probably the greatest expository preacher of his day, was our pastor for nine years. Although the teaching was wonderful, I lacked the power to live what I was being taught. After heading off in several wrong directions, the Lord caught up with me and graciously filled me with the Holy Spirit.

Prior to the baptism of the Holy Spirit, I remember being hungry to know Jesus in an intimate way. I longed to be lost in His presence and to experience His power. I felt He wanted that too. After being filled with the Spirit, I was delivered from several demonic strongholds in my life. Only then did I begin to have the relationship with God that I desired.

Still hungry to experience more of God, I read my Bible with a new eagerness. It became clear to me that there was another realm, another dimension of knowing God of which I was unaware. There is a right and a wrong kind of reasoning. When *reason* of heart becomes *treason* of heart, we are prevented from obeying God in faith (see Luke 5:22). The right kind of reasoning allows the Holy Spirit to bring light and revelation to us. Our minds can be fed by the Spirit of the Lord, the wisdom of this world, or spirits that pervert and distort the truth. All these want to captivate our minds. Paul instructed the Corinthians to "bring every thought into captivity to the obedience of Christ" (2 Cor. 10:5).

After spending all those years as a Christian with no real victory or joy, I said to God, "Thank You for filling me with Your Spirit and showing me that You are still moving in the earth today. But I don't want just to have more head knowledge. I want You to be real in my life. I don't walk around my house saying, 'I believe my husband is here! David *is* here!' I just know he is here, because *he is*."

Many people find themselves frustrated with all the Christian talk. They are tired of receiving more information, learning more Scripture verses and having more teaching. Increased knowledge is very wearisome if the Holy Spirit is missing. "The kingdom of God is not in word but in power" (1 Cor. 4:20).

Then God revealed something to me. Jesus left us with not only great information about God, but with an inheritance that would enable us to walk in the realms in which He walked. Many supernatural things happened in the life of the early church, including visions, Holy Spirit earthquakes, angelic visitations and supernatural salvation experiences. I believed those things were meant to be a part of my life as well. After a short while I started experiencing supernatural manifestations of the Holy Spirit. I was lifted into heaven several times, and I smelled the perfumes of the Lord as the Holy Spirit revealed the presence of Jesus. I experienced angelic visitations. Often the things of the Spirit realm became so strong that I couldn't tell them apart from the things of the natural realm.

The Holy Spirit moves in our faith; it is contrary to His nature to move in accordance with our unbelief. Jesus was not of this world, and neither are we who are born again. "Our citizenship is in heaven" (Phil. 3:20).

In the following chapters I will tell about some of the supernatural manifestations and outpourings of the Holy Spirit that my husband and I have had the privilege to experience. This book is meant to encourage you to receive this part of your inheritance as a child of God.

I get so angry with the devil for stealing from God's people. It makes me sad to see many Christians lacking God's power in their Christian experience. Jesus Christ is not a doctrine, the Holy Spirit is not an "it," and the Father is not a theology; all are Persons of the Godhead. You can't fellowship with or fall in love with a teaching.

The Scriptures are meant to bring us into a relationship with Jesus, but so often we stop with the words. Jesus said to the Pharisees, "Search the scriptures; for in them you think you have eternal life; and these are they which testify of Me. But you are not willing to come to Me that you might have life" (John 5:39,40).

Jesus wants a beautiful bride who loves Him, not one who merely knows about Him. The body of Christ is full of knowledge, but we need to be full of Jesus' presence also. We are to be filled with all the "fullness of Him who fills all in all" (Eph. 1:23). Stop thinking that the power of God is only for the man or woman on the platform. It is also for you, since you have been called by God into the body of Christ. "For the promise [of the Spirit] is to you and to your children, and to all who are afar off, as many as the Lord our God will call" (Acts 2:39).

TWO

PROVING GOD

In the early church, people spoke in other tongues and prophesied. Many were healed and delivered from evil spirits. Even a casual reader of the book of Acts can see these things happening again and again.

Our First Experience of Church

The more my husband and I read, the more we wanted this for ourselves. We had experienced only programmed meetings and traditional services. We had never learned how to listen to the voice of the Spirit. All our understanding came directly from our minds. We didn't understand Paul's letter to the Ephesians:

> Making mention of you in my prayers: that the God
> of our Lord Jesus Christ, the Father of glory, may
> give to you the spirit of wisdom and revelation in the
> knowledge of Him, the eyes of your understanding

> being enlightened; that you may know what is the
> hope of His calling, what are the riches of the glory
> of His inheritance in the saints (Eph. 1:16-18).

Finally, in a small gathering of friends, we gave ourselves completely to the Holy Spirit to do with us whatever He wanted. As we did, the power of God began to flow through the people gathered there. Because we had totally submitted our hearts and minds to the Holy Spirit, He was able to fill us with His power. After we were filled, the Holy Spirit began to wash our minds and filter out the head knowledge we had accumulated.

Sometimes during our praise and worship, the power of God would come upon us as Jesus' presence was manifested. People would slide to the floor and lay prostrate, sometimes for hours. On several occasions the young people left our house to walk to the bus stop, but they never made it. Drunk with "new wine," they toppled into the bushes! One night some of the youngsters fell into a neighbor's front yard, unable to move for almost an hour.

For two years we met in several homes around the town. Eventually we had to move into the local town hall for our main meetings. The meetings exploded spiritually. One Sunday morning a small boy started a chorus, and, as we sang, waves of the Spirit moved over the people. The people seemed to go one way and the chairs the other way. Two hundred people ended up flat on the floor! Two first-time visitors clung to their seats — they were the only ones left sitting.

Many of us were challenged to change our lives as we learned to move in the gifts of the Spirit. Hearts were touched and pierced. Though some men and women would have been happy with a religious discussion — keeping God at arm's length — the word of knowledge in operation made that impossible.

In the Gospel of John a woman from Samaria who came to draw water at a well where Jesus was resting tried to keep Him at a distance with a religious discussion. But this ordinary meeting was transformed into the supernatural as Jesus gave a word of knowledge to the woman about her five husbands! As Jesus continued speaking, not getting involved in her religious words, the woman finally recognized Him as the Messiah of Israel (see John 4: 6-26).

Most of the young people in our church had a desire to evangelize. They often went to the worst pub in our area where large numbers of drug pushers hung out. The young people stood outside as the druggies and pushers went into the pub. The Lord gave the Christian kids words of knowledge, and they offered to pray for the people. Many were saved and delivered right there on the street. Some of them eventually became pastors and elders in local churches.

Proving God in the Marketplace

After David and I were married I worked in the accounting department of a company in London. God's Spirit was moving, and many people came to our home fellowship. We knew it was only a matter of time before we went into full-time ministry. I was determined to leave that company with a great testimony.

The Spirit began to manifest His power in our office, and the people who worked there sensed the reality of the Lord. One of the things that caught the attention of the chief accountant and the staff was how the Lord moved on my behalf at the end of every month when we tried to balance the books. While everyone else was frantically poring over the huge ledger sheets looking for mistakes to correct, I would bow my head and pray, and the Holy Spirit would immediately tell me the error. Consequently, my books and accounts were balanced within a few minutes.

At one time there was a mail strike which was expected to last a couple of weeks. Since we were unable to send out monthly statements, no one bothered to prepare them for mailing. After a few days, the Holy Spirit told me to get the statements ready because the strike would be over in the morning. As I folded the statements and put them into envelopes, the assistant accountant asked me what I was doing.

"The Lord told me I can mail them in the morning," I replied. He just rolled his eyes in disbelief.

The next day's early morning news reported that the strike was over. I picked up my statements, hurried to the post office and was back by 9:20 A.M. When I returned, the chief accountant asked me if I would help the others prepare their mail.

A few weeks later there was an Asian flu epidemic in London. The symptoms lasted two to three weeks. The chief accountant arranged for everyone to get a flu shot, but I declined. "This flu shot is ninety percent proof," he angrily told me.

"Well, my protection is one hundred percent proof," I replied.

Later that afternoon I began to sneeze, my nose began to run, and my eyes were watering. When it was time to go home, my coworkers called out laughingly, "See you in a couple of weeks."

In the train on the way home I prayed, "This healing thing was Your idea, so now it's up to You, Lord. I must be fit for tomorrow." But I felt worse.

When I arrived home, I told my husband the situation, and he prayed for me. I was healed instantly. The next morning I arrived at work perfectly healthy, much to the amazement of the staff. Although they knew the Lord had healed me, they didn't want to acknowledge Him.

Then the Lord added to it with an experience that happened after I left the company. After four months of serving in full-time ministry I received a phone call from the chief accountant. "Kathie, we have a mistake somewhere in our sales accounts, and we cannot find it. We have looked and looked but with no luck. We thought that maybe you could help us find it. You could ask Him — you know, the Man up there — and He will tell you where it is." My old boss did not want to use the words "pray" or "God," but he was getting close. They were so desperate that he offered to pay me anything I wanted.

I knew this would be an excellent opportunity for God to manifest His power, so I agreed to come. The next day as I walked from the train station to the office, I said to the Lord, "Father! This is a great occasion for You to be glorified. They know that I am going to ask You where the mistake is, so I believe that You will show me right away."

When I walked into the office, I found they had placed about two hundred very large ledger sheets full of figures on a desk. It would normally take at least a week to sort through them.

The other people were seated at their desks, pretending to work, but they were watching me out of the corners of their eyes.

Bowing my head briefly, I prayed, "OK, Lord, now show me." I turned the sheets one at a time.

Suddenly the Holy Spirit said, "There it is in the middle of the page."

I immediately spotted the mistake and showed it to the chief accountant. No more than five minutes had passed since I began looking for the error. Everyone, including my ex-boss, was stunned. As he thanked me, I said, "Don't thank me. You know I couldn't have done that by myself."

Remember that the Holy Spirit in you knows all things. If you are open, He will give you words of knowledge so you can witness to others. It will not always be easy, and some people may think you are crazy for obeying the Holy Spirit. But whatever their reactions, never underestimate what can happen inside their spirits.

I remember going to a grocery store where a girl was bagging the groceries in the line next to mine. She was not in a good mood. The Holy Spirit said, "She is rebelling against someone in authority in her life. Tell her this person only wants what is good for her. I have placed that person in her life."

I began a debate with the Lord. But I have since learned that whenever I do that, I never win! "Lord, if she comes out the same door I do, I'll know You want me to talk to her." Relieved that she went out the other door, I determined to pray for her that night.

As I walked toward my car, the Holy Spirit prompted me again. "I asked you to tell her."

"If she is on my side of the store when I go back in," I said, "I will know that You actually want me to speak to her." I went back inside, and she went out the opposite door, talking to the customer with her. I was relieved.

But as I walked back toward my car, she suddenly headed in my direction. I knew that if I continued to disobey the Holy Spirit, every time I went to that store I would remember my unwillingness to follow the Lord's directions.

I took a deep breath and walked toward her. "Excuse me," I said. "I am a Christian, and I believe the Lord has given me a word for you."

She looked as though she wanted to smack me, but I continued to tell her what the Holy Spirit had shown me. Her face changed, and she began to cry right there in the parking lot.

"I am a Christian, too," she said. "My youth pastor has been trying so hard to minister to me, but I have rebelled against everything he's tried to do. Tonight at my youth meeting I will ask him to forgive me."

I was so grateful that I had obeyed the Holy Spirit.

On another occasion, my husband and I were eating lunch in a very pleasant but crowded restaurant. After finally being seated, I noticed that the table next to ours had twelve people seated around it. They were giving the waitress a very hard time. The more difficult they were, the more upset the waitress became.

When something wasn't right about the order, one man lost his temper and yelled at her. The embarrassed girl turned away quickly, causing every waitress's nightmare: She dropped the tray of food!

My heart went out to her. I saw tears begin to run down her face as she bent down under the table to pick up the tray. I crawled under the table and smiled as I helped her pick up the food. Then I prayed a simple prayer for God's peace to be evident.

As the peace of the Lord came, she smiled and sweetly attended to the angry people at the table. They calmed down and were apologetic for their uncivilized behavior.

As we were leaving the restaurant she came running out, her eyes shining. "Thank you so much for praying," she said. "I am a backslidden Christian, and my father is a pastor. All week the Lord has been telling me to go back, make things right and fulfill the call of God on my life. This was a confirmation that He still loves me." What a blessing to see God's love manifested to this girl. God wants us to be a channel of His blessing.

Doing Nothing but Accomplishing Everything

Jesus stated, "I can of Myself do nothing" (John 5:30). "The Son can do nothing of Himself, but what He sees the Father do" (John 5:19). He also said, "Without Me you can do nothing" (John 15:5). Though He said that He could do nothing of Himself, He proceeded to do everything.

Jesus Christ spoke — and then demonstrated. He said, "I am the light of the world," then He opened the eyes of the blind (see John 8:12; Luke 7:21). He said, "I am the bread of life," then He fed the five thousand (see John 6:35; Matt. 14:19-21). He said, "I am the resurrection and the life," then He raised the dead (see John 11:25, 43-44). He came not only to teach but also to do (see Acts 1:1).

The apostle Paul declared, "For the kingdom of God is not in word but in power" (1 Cor. 4:20). Why? This power demonstrates the kingdom of God. This is the kingdom of which Jesus spoke to the disciples and to the New Testament church. God bears witness to the gospel and the preaching of the good news, "both with signs and wonders, with various miracles, and gifts of the Holy Spirit, according to His own will" (Heb. 2:4).

We are not to promote a lesser gospel than Jesus preached; nor are we to offer a weak, diluted demonstration of God's goodness and grace. God's promises are yes and amen. He is not a yes-and-no God of inconsistencies.

> For the Son of God, Jesus Christ, who was preached among you by us — by me Silvanus, and Timothy — was not Yes and No, but in Him was Yes. For all the promises of God in Him are Yes, and in Him Amen, to the glory of God through us (2 Cor. 1:19-20).

THREE

OUR INHERITANCE

If someone notified you that you were to receive an inheritance, you would be curious to know what that inheritance was. We are told in the Word of God that Jesus, our elder brother, died and left an inheritance for us (Eph. 1:11,14; Acts 20:32).

Jesus' most important possession was a wonderful relationship with the Father. He fellowshipped with and knew the Father intimately. Jesus had the same mind and heart as His Father did, and as we yield our will to His will, we can too. "I in them, and You in Me; that they may be made perfect in one, and that the world may know that You have sent Me, and have loved them as you have loved Me" (John 17:23).

Eternal life is also included in this inheritance. "I give them eternal life, and they shall never perish; neither shall anyone snatch them out of My hand" (John 10:28).

Suppose your attorney read you only part of a will? Or what if many things had been given to you and your family that you never knew about because you tucked the will away in a drawer somewhere? Satan tries to hide from us the reality of our inheritance in Jesus.

When Jesus began His ministry, religious spirits blinded many people's eyes just as they do today. For my first nine years as a Christian, I was blinded in many areas. I knew about only part of my salvation — I didn't know anything about Jesus' provision for my healing, the baptism of the Spirit or the gifts of the Spirit.

Paul wrote, "The gospel...is the power of God to salvation for everyone who believes" (Rom. 1:16). We are to have the same quality of life that Jesus had. It's our inheritance. We are to walk as Jesus walked — in communion with the Father. The life of the Father flowed through Him, conquering demons, sickness, death, hate and even false religion.

But the devil tries to deceive us with religious spirits which rob the people of God. Even "good" can become the enemy of God. We often accept that which is merely good and miss God's best. Religious spirits aren't intimidated by the form of service or program we have. They don't care what kind of Bible study we attend — as long as *God's life* isn't flowing in *us*. We can do as many works as we want to as long as the Holy Spirit doesn't show up and start manifesting the life of Christ to people.

When my husband, David, preached in the public schools in England, no one minded when he gave little talks on Christianity. But when the Holy Spirit began to move, and the kids repented, wept and got healed, then the demons got mad. The apostle Paul said, "My speech and my preaching were not with persuasive words of human wisdom, but in demonstration of the Spirit and of power" (1 Cor. 2:4). This demonstration of power is also our inheritance.

I love to see signs and wonders. I love to see the things my heavenly Father can do. I delight in it, for there is nothing more wonderful than to be where God's Spirit is moving with a demonstration of the awesomeness of His love and power.

Jesus reached multitudes in a short time. How did He always know what was happening in the spirit realm? How did He speak words that pierced the hearts of the people and met all their needs? He always knew their motives. He operated in peace and confidence. He listened to the voice of His Father and was led by the Holy Spirit in all He did.

Jesus wasn't governed by the natural realm; He was governed by what the Father said. A good example occurred when Lazarus's sisters sent Jesus a message telling Him their brother was very sick. The Bible tells us that Jesus loved Lazarus.

You or I would have dropped everything and caught the first bus, train or plane to get there as quickly as possible. But Jesus didn't go anywhere for two days. "When He [Jesus] heard that he was sick, He stayed two more days in the place where He was" (John 11:6). I can imagine the people around him saying to each other, "I thought Jesus loved Lazarus! He doesn't seem to care very much. He isn't even going to see him."

But Jesus was not motivated by the things His ears heard or even by the needs of the people. He was motivated by the voice of His Father. He stayed until His Father released Him to go.

Until we learn to discern, listen to and obey the Spirit, we will just stumble around, trying to help others in our own strength through the natural realm. We will experience a major victory in our lives when we learn to minister through the power of the Holy Spirit, who brings life into every circumstance.

After waiting for two days, Jesus went to Judea, telling his disciples that Lazarus was dead (v. 14). It probably seemed pointless to the disciples to make the trip, yet they went with Him. Upon arriving at Lazarus's home in Bethany, Jesus learned that His friend had been dead for four days. The first comment of Martha, Lazarus's sister, was, "Lord, if You had been here, my brother would not have died" (John 11:21). Her faith was limited, and He said to her, "Your brother will rise again" (v. 23). Then she spoke about the "resurrection at the last day" (v. 24). Her faith was in the future, not the present — and it was actually just hope, not faith. Mary repeated what her sister had said (v. 32). So Jesus heard with His ears that He was too late. When they rolled away the stone from the tomb, His eyes told Him that He was too late. And when He smelled the stench of the body, His nose also told him that He was too late!

Everything in the natural realm gave Jesus information. But He was not motivated by the natural, rather by the voice of the Father (see Is. 11:3). He obeyed that voice, saying, "Lazarus, come forth!" (v. 43). And immediately "he who had died came out" (v. 44).

The natural realm may shout the loudest, but the Holy Spirit has more authority than the natural realm. Do you want to learn to live in the Spirit and walk in the Spirit? Do you want to live in the realm of the miraculous, see the anointing of God, talk to the angels, have the Holy Spirit lift you into the heavenlies and reveal Jesus to you? Then there is only one way. Learn to feed from the tree of life, which is Christ Jesus.

My husband and I, along with others from our church, prayed for a young lady named Pamela who was a diabetic. She was healed and delivered. Several months went by, and she had no problems. One day she came to our home to tell us that the symptoms of diabetes had returned. David asked her if she could think of anything which might have caused the door to be open for this sickness to return. She insisted there was no sin, no reason she could think of. The Holy Spirit showed us that she had unforgiveness in her heart, but she insisted that she did not.

Some other friends came to our home, and we prepared supper. Suddenly David turned to Pamela and said, "Whom do you blame for your diabetes?"

She cried out, "It was my mother's fault. She dropped me when I was a small child, and I went into shock.[1] After that I became a diabetic." There was no need for us to say anything since the tone of her voice spoke louder than all her denials. She finally repented. We prayed again, and she was healed — this time permanently. The Holy Spirit is able to deliver, but we must learn to listen to His voice.

---

[1]There have been several known cases in which a sudden shock has caused the pancreas to cease functioning, resulting in diabetes.

FOUR

LEARNING TO KNOW THE HOLY SPIRIT

The truth and reality of Jesus are revealed to us by the Holy Spirit as He leads, guides and teaches us. Before I was baptized in the Holy Spirit, I felt as if I did not really know Him. Oh, I knew *about* Him, but I didn't have an intimate relationship with Him. But seeing His works and feeling His awesome presence gripped me with a passion to know Him. I asked Him to teach me His ways, to show me the things He liked and those that grieved Him. Some things we know only in our minds. But He reveals things to our hearts as He teaches us, and they affect our whole lives.

The Holy Spirit is a spirit of truth. If we are to have an intimate relationship with Him, we must recognize that there can be no pretense with Him. Truth has to be acceptable to us even though it's often easier not to hear it. We must love the truth; it's the essence of His nature.

Walking with the Holy Spirit requires devotion. God is the only One who has a right to demand our unquestioning loyalty.

Although others may require or ask it of us, no matter how great or worthy a person may seem to be, we cannot give unquestioning loyalty. All men are fallible and vulnerable to making errors. Many people of God are confused on this issue.

Our work, church, ministry or pastor cannot be placed above the Holy Spirit in this matter of loyalty. We must support, love and care for our leaders, but if we put them in the place reserved for God, we will end up in trouble — and so will they. Many great ministries that have been worshipped for their giftings have come falling down. Their Christian followers were also to blame for lifting them up higher than where God had placed them in the Spirit.

The Holy Spirit is part of the Godhead. God is a jealous God. It is important to realize that the Holy Spirit is also jealous if we give our affections or total loyalty to anyone or anything else apart from Jesus. He wants us to love Him and fellowship with Him. He wants us to listen to His voice first, to rely on Him so much that we do nothing without Him. We must learn to listen to the Spirit in our hearts, waiting to see what He says before we make commitments. We must learn to be led by the Spirit and not be motivated by need.

When someone tells you of a problem or need, remember to listen first to what the Holy Spirit is saying about it. Do what He wants you to do in response. He knows the motives and intents of each person's heart — you don't (see Heb. 4:12). His voice will become stronger in your spirit as you obey His promptings.

Learning to Hear

Many of us in the body of Christ have a great desire to hear the Holy Spirit's voice and move out in faith. We want to be a blessing, but we are fearful of making a mistake or of missing His voice. Not wanting to look foolish, we decide to do nothing rather than risk taking actions prompted by the Holy Spirit. We take ourselves too seriously most of the time. It puts a heavy burden on us to make everything go right. Many things are beyond our control — God is ultimately in control. He is the only One able to change hearts.

Everything is in perfect order in a graveyard, but no one moves either. I choose a life with a few messes rather than death (see Prov. 14:4). When a toddler first learns to walk, he falls over many times. But he doesn't just lie on the ground saying, "I will never try this again; this walking stuff doesn't work for me." A toddler pulls himself up and tries again, falling many more times. It may take several days before he makes it across the room. Don't be afraid to make a mistake as you learn to walk in the Spirit. You won't lose your salvation. God will still love you.

In our first Spirit-filled church, we wanted to learn to hear God's voice and step out in faith. But none of us had ever been so bold before. All this "hearing from God" stuff was brand new to us, but we were determined to try.

Frank, one of our young men, decided to learn to hear the voice of the Holy Spirit and step out in faith. Late one evening he felt the Holy Spirit prompting him to make sandwiches and hot coffee for the street people who slept on the benches down by the river. His wife, Anita, wasn't too encouraging, as the ingredients he took for the sandwiches were to be used for dinner the next day.

Undeterred, Frank rode off on his bicycle. It was a foggy, cold and damp night just like those in old English movies. Frank arrived and sat down on one of the benches with sandwiches and coffee intact. He sat there for three hours with no one in sight. There wasn't a soul anywhere. By this time Frank was cold, hungry and thirsty. Eventually he realized that even street people had more sense than to be out on such a miserable night, so he sat and ate the sandwiches himself.

When he related his experience to me, I asked him what happened.

"I tried to walk in the Spirit and fell," he responded. But Frank didn't quit. He got up, laughed at himself and kept on walking.

It was wonderful to watch people in our fellowship learning to hear from God regarding their giving. Sometime later I invited a local pastor and his wife over for a spaghetti dinner. The table was laid and the salad prepared, and I was about to serve the spaghetti. Suddenly I realized that I had completely forgotten about meat sauce. One can hardly serve up great piles of spaghetti with nothing at all to go on it. I was very embarrassed. These guests were not close friends. We were hoping to witness to them about the baptism of the Holy Spirit.

"Oh, Lord," I prayed, "what now?"

Just at that moment there was a knock on the door. On the step was one of the elders holding a white dish with a cover over it. "Thirty minutes ago the Holy Spirit told my wife to make this for you," he said. He put the dish into my hands and jumped back into his car. In the white dish was enough meat sauce for the four of us. Our guests never knew how close they came to having a very bland dinner!

As you learn to walk in the supernatural, you may stumble. If at first you don't succeed, don't quit — try again. A lot of us have spent most of our lives not listening to God. It takes a little while to "tune in" to Him. Be patient and don't give up — you will get it right. The Holy Spirit will encourage you. He desires to use you.

A friend with a great faith-healing ministry in England and throughout the world once said, "When I began praying for the sick, the first three people I prayed for died. I thought I had a ministry of death! But then I said to the Lord, 'Your word says that they will lay hands on the sick and they will recover (Mark 16:18). So I don't care if I never see anyone healed. I will continue to pray, because You said it in Your word." Needless to say it was not long before the Lord gave him a miraculous healing ministry.

FIVE

YIELDING TO THE HOLY SPIRIT

The Holy Spirit draws and woos us. Our responsibility is to respond to Him. As we yield, He will do the things that are necessary for our growth.

There is a scripture that Satan twists to try to confuse us: "Walk in the Spirit, and you shall not fulfill the lust of the flesh" (Gal. 5:16). Before my husband was filled with the Spirit, he spent years trying not to fulfill the lust of the flesh in order to qualify to walk in the Spirit. It was an impossible goal.

That is not the Holy Spirit's way. The verse says that if we walk in the Spirit, we will not fulfill the lust of the flesh. The emphasis is on walking in the Spirit — and the "will not" becomes a promise. The works of the flesh are initiated by the flesh, whether they be good, bad or religious. They can appear outwardly to be good — like the Pharisees. Outwardly they did good works, but Jesus called them "whited sepulchres." The works were not the Holy Spirit's works, and the fruit was not His fruit. It was not initiated by the Spirit.

We read this account of the children of Israel in Hebrews 4: "They to whom it was first preached entered not in because of unbelief...he that is entered into His rest, he also hath ceased from his own works, as God did from His" (vv. 6,10, KJV). Isn't that wonderful? What a relief! We do not have to produce our own works any longer. It is a matter of simply letting the Holy Spirit have His way in our lives.

Imagine being in Moses' shoes (see Ex. 14). He was in charge of all the people of Israel. They had left Egypt and were by the seashore. Pharaoh, with all of his army, horses and chariots, came thundering after them. There was nowhere to go: The Red Sea was in front, and Pharaoh was behind. They were trapped and afraid.

In the natural realm the only thing for Moses to do would be to shout, "Run for your life! Every man for himself!" But Moses said, "Do not be afraid. Stand still...." That sounds extremely ridiculous to the natural mind. But Moses wasn't finished speaking. He continued, "...and see the salvation of the Lord" (Ex. 14:13). Moses had to put down his own arm of strength because there was nothing he could do.

Then God said something very wonderful: "The Lord will fight for you, and you shall hold your peace" (v. 14). When Moses rested, God told him what to do. He said, "Tell the children of Israel to go forward" (v. 15). The only place forward was the Red Sea. How ridiculous that sounds to the natural man. But God said, "[Moses,] lift up your rod, and stretch out your hand over the sea and divide it" (v. 16). The people went through on dry land in the midst of the sea. What a great supernatural victory!

This is God's way. He did it. "His right hand and His holy arm have gained Him the victory" (Ps. 98:1). As soon as Moses was totally dependent upon God, God used His arm to part the sea. Moses was blessed to be a part of the miracle. God wants to use us in supernatural ways, but He cannot use the arm of our flesh. Learn to rest in Him and believe that He "is able to do exceedingly abundantly above all that we ask or think, according to the power that works in us" (Eph. 3:20).

The Anointing

We must yield to the Spirit and let Him initiate the works. If they are initiated by Him, they will be anointed; if they are not, there will be no anointing upon them.

Only the anointing can destroy the yoke of flesh. Merely breaking the yoke is not enough; that which is broken can be repaired, but that which is destroyed is finished. We must desire and seek the anointing. God will never anoint the flesh or man-made programs, because "no flesh should glory in His presence" (1 Cor. 1:29). God is not interested in religious superstars even though many Christians are. True unity in the body of Christ only comes through the Spirit. Not even man's attempts through religious or ecclesiastical rules or agreements in doctrine or theology can bring unity.

The psalmist says, "Behold, how good and how pleasant it is for brethren to dwell together in unity! It is like the precious oil upon the head, running down on the beard, the beard of Aaron, running down on the edge of his garments" (Ps. 133:1-2). The oil never touched the flesh. It went on his head, then down his beard and onto his garments. God will not anoint our old fleshly ways. Jesus said, "No one puts new wine into old wineskins" (Mark 2:22).

SIX

THE HOLY SPIRIT'S VISITATION

During a Sunday service at our church, a guest minister suddenly spoke a word by the Spirit: "Are you going to push through the crowd like the woman who touched the hem of Jesus's garment?"

The Holy Spirit sent that word right to my heart, and I responded, "Oh, yes, Lord. Whatever that means in my life, I want to press right through the crowd."

Each one of us has our own personal "crowd." That crowd consists of things that keep you from touching Jesus. My crowd may not be the same as yours, although some things may be similar. The crowd in your life may be television, or it may be people you have placed before God in your loyalty and affection. It may be golf, sports or even your ministry. But if you ask the Holy Spirit, He will show you the crowd. Then you have to be determined to push past it and move it out of the way. You must be aggressive. Whatever captures so much of your attention that you think you can't live without it is the bondage which must be broken.

Religious bondage can be very deceptive and difficult to discern. Two of our Christian friends, Mac and Pauline, were members of the church we attended before we became aware of the Holy Spirit's power. Pauline had suffered through several miscarriages and was pregnant again.

One morning she called us on the phone to ask us to pray. She felt that another miscarriage was starting to happen. She had received prayer for healing but to no avail.

Ian Andrews, a friend who had been ministering nearby, dropped in to see us. We sought his insight on the situation, telling him about the miscarriages and the failure of our prayers for healing.

"I believe she needs deliverance," he told us, "not healing. You need to rebuke the spirit of infirmity which has come down through her family tree and is causing those miscarriages." He encouraged us to pray for her as soon as possible.

We called to tell Pauline that we were coming over to pray with her. By the time we arrived, the Lord had given her this verse: "Whoever calls on the name of the Lord shall be saved" (Joel 2:32). We prayed and rebuked the spirit of infirmity just as Jesus had done (see Luke 13:11,12). After several minutes a demon manifested itself. Pauline went into convulsions. Soon the spirit left, and Pauline began to weep and rejoice. "I know everything is going to be fine" she said. (Later she gave birth to a seven-and-a-half-pound baby with no problems.)

At that time her husband, Mac, arrived home from work. He did not know what had happened, so Pauline excitedly related her experience to him.

David suggested that we pray together before we left. The four of us stood in the middle of the room to pray. Mac was considered by many to be a very spiritual man. He had been well taught in the Scriptures for many years and probably knew the Bible better than most of us.

As we stood together praising the Lord, the Holy Spirit suddenly gave me a vision of a piece of white typing paper in a typewriter, with the words "Love you" on it. I shared how the vision made the words seem very impersonal.

Suddenly David turned toward Mac and spoke to the spirit within him: "You cold, hard, religious spirit, come out of him."

Mac looked up, then closed his eyes and slowly sank to the floor, doubled over. We all stared in disbelief. David could hardly believe his own voice. After a few minutes Mac arose looking a little shaken, but he seemed fine, and we went home.

What happened next is very important. Mac was a good person. He knew all the right doctrines and had lived all his life among Christians. But when that religious spirit left him, he had no desire to serve God anymore. He never attended another prayer meeting or any other kind of Christian meeting after that day. He didn't want to because he wasn't interested. He was still a nice, kind person, but he wasn't a Christian. Apparently he never had been one.

We often judge so much by what we see and hear in the natural. All of us assumed that Mac must be a Christian because he was so good and knew so much about the Bible. But Mac apparently just had a religious spirit. Non-Christians can be very nice people. But being nice, kind, generous and religious isn't the issue. People can have so much religious or biblical knowledge that they constantly amaze you, but that isn't the issue, either.

The question is, do they love Jesus? Have they established a relationship with the Father? Mac later told us that he had never had a relationship with the Lord. But no one challenged him, so he continued in this way for years until the Holy Spirit shone His light on the situation.

I was still seeking the Lord concerning the word He gave about "pushing through the crowd." During that time, many people who needed accommodations were staying at our house. David was away preaching in churches and schools in different parts of the country, and a teacher friend named Sheila was spending her summer vacation with me. Three young men were also temporarily staying at our home. One was an architect who was between jobs. The other two worked for themselves in a small business.

During a three-day period we felt impressed to wait on the Lord in prayer. We ate very little since we spent most of the time praying. We were not on a planned fast; we simply forgot to eat.

The Holy Spirit began to reveal areas in each individual's life where there were bondages. These were not major sins, just small things, but we recognized idolatry as the real problem. As God revealed these changes, each of us put things right with the Lord. While we were praying late one evening, there was a sudden sense of the Holy Spirit's presence in the room.

The Holy Spirit said, "Jesus is now where He should be."

Suddenly a noise like a wind came into the house. We all sat up with eyes wide open, not speaking, but excited and a little scared. The wind rushed around the room and suddenly fell on one of the young men. He began to experience deliverance as the Holy Spirit filled him. Then the wind went to the next person, and the same thing happened. It continued for several hours until everyone had been set free by the Holy Spirit.

Finally a strange thing happened. We could see and hear in the spiritual realm just as we could in the natural. Then an even stranger thing happened! Some demons came banging and knocking on the windows. They were screeching and making all kinds of noises. We felt they were just trying to frighten us and make us stop seeking the Lord. They must have been there before, but we hadn't been able to see them. We just went to bed (although Sheila did ask if she could share my room for the night). In the morning the demons were gone, and a great peace filled the house.

There is no substitute for the Holy Spirit. He is the only One who knows all things. The Holy Spirit will call you, speak to you and draw you so that you will yield to Him.

Sometimes we behave as if He isn't doing anything, as if He's nowhere around. We think He is not interested in us. But that's a lie; He is always present. He loves to reveal Jesus to His people. We can't change ourselves or others. "But we all, with unveiled face, beholding as in a mirror the glory of the Lord, are being transformed into the same image from glory to glory, just as by the Spirit of the Lord" (2 Cor. 3:18).

SEVEN

DISCERNING BY THE SPIRIT

One early lesson the Holy Spirit taught us was the difference between human sympathy and compassion. Sympathy is a natural human reaction to need. But it will not set people free from their problems, whether these problems are bondage, loss, depression or sickness in any form.

The Holy Spirit gives compassion. Real compassion produces righteousness, and God's righteousness will produce action. The Holy Spirit's actions are always released to bring people to the truth. Jesus said, "The truth shall make you free" (John 8:32). It will free a person from sin, death and all of death's works.

Bondage is the work of death. Fear, sin, disease, worry and emotional or financial needs will keep us from the liberty Jesus promised in the Spirit (see Rom. 8:21; 2 Cor. 3:17).

This area of loyalty to the voice and leading of the Holy Spirit will always be tested. Old habits or patterns of behavior will cause you to react to need without asking God to show you what is going on in the Spirit.

Before we knew how to minister according to the Spirit, we visited a small church located in a tiny village called South Chard in Somerset County in the southwest of England. The Spirit of the Lord was moving mightily in that church. People's lives were being touched. We were very excited but apprehensive, as we didn't really understand anything about the ways of the Spirit. After supper we attended the Saturday evening meeting along with many visitors from England, Sweden, Iceland, Holland, Germany and the United States.

We were early, so there was time for some fellowship before the meeting started. We were introduced to a few people by our friends Ralph and Michele. David and I noticed a young lady sitting by herself and crying. No one seemed to notice, and I felt sorry for her. I thought, What is the matter with these people? They are supposed to be so spiritual; how can they just ignore this poor girl?

I sat next to her, putting my arm around her. She continued to cry and mumbled something about how bad she felt. She complained that no one loved her. I didn't really know what to do or how to minister to her except to offer my sympathy.

I tried to call my friend Ralph over, but he just smiled and continued to talk to someone else. Then the pastor came by and said, "Leave her alone. God is dealing with her, and she will be delivered before the weekend is over." We were a little shocked, but we did as he said. The poor girl looked miserable all through the meeting.

When we were back at our friend's house after the meeting, I asked why no one had ministered to the young lady. Ralph and Michele explained to us that she had received some ministry and deliverance earlier that afternoon. But the key to her total deliverance would be for her to give up her self-pity and get her life focused on Jesus and His will for her. The spirit of self-pity had been in her since she was a small child. She had used the spirit in order to gain attention, and it was a battle for her to let it go. But doing that was a decision only the person involved could make.

The next morning in the Sunday service I was amazed to see the girl worshipping the Lord with all her heart. The joy of the Lord was shining through her, and she received a mighty deliverance and baptism in the Spirit. She was later used very effectively among the young people in Sweden.

I really learned something from that experience. Sympathy will not set anyone free, but the truth will. If you sympathize with sickness, your sympathy will never bring healing. If you sympathize with religious spirits, people will not come out of dryness. A compassionate heart learns how to minister the truth motivated by love.

That same weekend I received my baptisms. I was baptized by immersion for the first time. I also received a mighty baptism in the Holy Spirit. I was unable to stop speaking in tongues. During that weekend we were amazed to see so many speaking out in prophecy, giving words of knowledge and messages in tongues, telling about visions and revelations, and ministering the Word. The ministry of the Word was not a formal, planned message prepared by a pastor. Several people ministered and brought forth the Word of God. The Holy Spirit orchestrated the entire series of meetings.

The pastor was a little man who sat at the back of the church, preaching only occasionally. When he did minister, he stood on a chair and, with tears running down his face, preached about the love and presence of Jesus. All this had a profound effect upon me. It gave David and me a hunger to know Jesus and the Holy Spirit in the way the pastor was describing. Although the church had only about 150 members, it had eight full-time ministers. These men and women lived by faith, traveling in England and abroad to minister in conferences, churches and home fellowships. The pastor encouraged us to have regular meetings in our hometown.

Ministering to the Needy, Not to Needs

It is a good thing to give money to the poor. But if that's all you give, it will not ultimately help the person to whom you are ministering. During the early seventies we preached in the villages of Kenya where the people are poor. After giving away most of our money, the Lord gave me a dream about fruit and vegetables. At first I didn't understand, but then the Lord gave David understanding from Joel 2:22-32. We began to break the spirit of the locust, the cankerworm and the devourer.

Most of them were growing only millet (a rough grain, heavy in starch) from which they made bread. Yet their land was fertile and could grow many kinds of vegetables and fruit. They lived under a poverty curse passed down from their ancestors, looking for Westerners to bail them out with handouts. We encouraged them to grow a variety of fruit and vegetables not only to improve their diets, but also to sell at the local markets. We told them how to pen their chickens in order to have eggs available, rather than searching all day for one or two eggs.

We must teach the poor to walk in the Lord's provision and to give to others. They can be led by the Spirit to become a channel of God's blessing.

Many people with compassionate hearts try to minister to people's needs rather than pointing them to the Lord. It's very hard not to respond immediately when people cry out for help. We saw an illustration of that in the story of the death of Lazarus. If people expect us to meet their needs, they will never develop a faith relationship with God. They will always be dependent upon others for healing, finances or counseling.

A minister friend of mine who could hear God in a remarkable way once said, "I would not give a penny to a beggar unless the Lord told me to." Most Christians are unable to discern the Lord's leading to that degree. This is not to suggest that you close your heart to the needy, as the priest and the Levite did on the Jericho road (Luke 10:30-37). It is always best to give and minister to those in need unless the Lord clearly tells you not to. As long as you are open to His leading, God will direct and guide you in this difficult area.

There is a fine line between the concept "If I don't save the world, nobody will" (what is often called a messiah complex) and "The Lord can do it just as well without us," or "He does it

anyway, in spite of our puny efforts." It is important ̄
learn to flow in the Holy Spirit in our everyday lives, an
ing with joy what the Lord has in store for us.

The Fella in the Cellar and the Fanatic in the Attic

We have a wonderful friend, Arthur Burt, who was a contemporary of Smith Wigglesworth. He has ministered to the body of Christ for at least forty years. This man was used greatly by God to teach us the ways of the Spirit. He explained the makeup of our beings in this way.

Each of us is like a house. We each have a spirit that is made alive by the Holy Spirit of God. We call that spirit the "fanatic in the attic." This fanatic can see from the heights and around corners with unlimited vision from its bird's eye view.

Each of us also has a mind, which may be brilliant in the natural realm. We call it the "fella in the cellar" because it cannot see above ground level; it cannot see in the spirit. The fella in the cellar knows nothing about the future and can only make decisions according to its sense knowledge. It is a servant but would like to be the boss.

There also is the "guy in the middle"— the heart or soul. The heart must decide which to follow — the fella in the cellar that shouts the loudest or the fanatic in the attic. The fanatic in the attic sees in the spirit and wants to follow God's call, but the fella in the cellar with its limited sight fearfully struggles against the fanatic.

The heart will have to choose which to obey. As we grow in the Lord and begin to delight in His will, our hearts will learn to follow after the spirit. Thus the mind realm bows to third place but eventually becomes enlightened with revelation. The spirit allows the light to enter, and the revelation reaches the mind with illumination.

Arthur related a true story to illustrate this idea. One rainy Sunday afternoon he was traveling by bus between two towns in the English countryside. The rain is always cold in England, and buses run infrequently, often with a two-hour wait between.

Suddenly Arthur's spirit said, "Arthur, get off the bus at the next stop."

His mind immediately responded, "You must be mad. You're in the middle of nowhere, and it's pouring rain. That was not the Spirit of God speaking to you; it was your imagination."

His spirit spoke again: "Arthur, get off the bus at the next stop."

Again that voice from the cellar prodded, "But there won't be another bus for two hours. Are you mad?"

Arthur's heart was left to choose which voice to obey. If he did not press the bell, the bus would not stop. Arthur jumped up and pressed the bell, and the driver stopped the bus. It pulled away leaving Arthur standing in the pouring rain. His mind shouted, "That wasn't God speaking to you — now you're in a mess. You'll get soaked to the skin while you wait two hours for the next bus."

But a few minutes later a passing car screeched to a halt and a voice said, "Brother Arthur, this must be God!" He recognized a young lady whom he knew. "Get in!" she said. "We are on our way to Brother Cecil Stuart's meeting. Will you come with us?"

When they arrived, Cecil saw Arthur and said, "Brother Burt has arrived. I believe God has sent him to preach to us tonight." Arthur preached with a great anointing that evening.

Many exciting adventures await those who let the fanatic in the attic lead the way. We must learn to listen and obey the voice of the Holy Spirit.

EIGHT

THE JUDGMENTS OF THE LORD ARE TRUE

The Holy Spirit is the only one who knows the intents and motivations of the heart. "The judgments of the Lord are true and righteous altogether" (Ps. 19:9).

Isaiah prophesied of Jesus, "His delight is in the fear of the Lord, and He shall not judge by the sight of His eyes, nor decide by the hearing of the ears; but with righteousness He shall judge the poor" (Is. 11:3-4).

Jesus said, "I can of Myself do nothing. As I hear, I judge; and My judgment is righteous, because I do not seek My own will but the will of the Father who sent Me" (John 5:30). He also warned, "Do not judge according to appearance, but judge with righteous judgment" (John 7:24). Jesus Christ did not make personal judgments, but He allowed the Father, who knows the secrets of hearts, to make the judgments.

The apostle Paul stated, "He who is spiritual judges all things" (1 Cor. 2:15). Who is "he who is spiritual"? Is it the one who knows all the Scriptures? No, religious demons can quote reams of Scripture verses.

Is it one who prays a lot? Not necessarily, but it certainly helps. Some pray out of a religious mind rather than according to the direction of the Holy Spirit. But all true prayer is initiated by the Holy Spirit, who knows what to pray for and how to pray for it and who always gets a response from God.

The spiritual person is the one who is learning to walk like Christ, depending on the Father and waiting to hear from heaven. He does not depend on the seeing of the natural eye or the hearing of the natural ear.

While living in England we made several ministry trips to the United States. On one trip we visited a very sweet group of Christians located on the outskirts of a Southern city. The church consisted of several small home groups that met twice a week, with all the groups meeting together twice a month. During the week we would minister in the smaller meetings. On one Sunday we had been invited to speak at a large home group since there was no general meeting. One of the elders offered to introduce us to the home-group leader.

As we arrived at the home of the elder on Saturday evening, he came to the door to greet us. He smiled pleasantly and seemed very nice, but when I shook his hand and looked into his eyes, I was flabbergasted to see a spirit of adultery looking straight at me.

Several people were in the room, and I tried to join in the conversation; but my thoughts were totally out of control. I was amazed to see Arthur Burt sitting in the chair to my right, sipping orange juice and talking with a young man. I thought, Well, Arthur Burt, I thought you were so spiritual. How can you just sit there and not do anything?

Time passed, with everyone still chatting and drinking their coffee and juice. Suddenly, Arthur put down his orange juice and gave a very loud message in tongues, which was followed by the interpretation. It was something like this: "God will reveal all things and bring everything into the light." Then he continued drinking his juice and talking as if nothing had happened.

When I returned to the home where we were staying, the Lord gave me understanding about the situation. God had graciously given the man an opportunity to repent. He had spoken to the man's heart through His Word, through a friend and finally through the Holy Spirit. Because he refused to hear and obey, God's judgment was now bringing the sin into the light.

God had been unable to use me because I judged the man in my own heart when I saw the spirit of adultery. My judgment was not righteous or full of compassion. But Arthur did not make that kind of judgment; he waited until the Spirit of the Lord spoke through him.

Why did Jesus spend time with the harlot but did not try to persuade the rich young ruler to follow Him? It has to do with the heart. He alone knows the heart. King David sinned greatly by committing adultery, lying and murdering Bathsheba's husband, Uriah the Hittite. But when confronted by Nathan (2 Sam. 12), he confessed and repented. God referred to David as one "who kept my commandments and who followed Me with all his heart, to do only what was right in my eyes" (1 Kin. 14:8).

If you have judged anyone according to your own judgment, repent and ask the Lord to reveal His heart for that ministry or person before you try to fellowship with the Holy Spirit.

If you have been judged with a false standard by another person or by a church, first forgive them and break the spirit of false judgment and false standards over you. Even God's standards, if given in a legalistic spirit, do not manifest the heart of God, because they do not contain His grace.

When you receive a word from the Lord for someone, and it contains correction or rebuke, be sure that your own emotions and biases are not involved. Wait on the Lord. Jesus never reacted; rather He always acted under the direction of the Holy Spirit. If you react, your emotions will distort the word of the Lord, even though what you say may contain some truth. A correction will become an accusation.

If someone has judged you wrongly, and you want to set him straight, wait on the Lord. He will tell you whether to keep silent or to speak.

NINE

AMAZING GRACE

W e are saved by faith in God's wonderful grace. We come to the cross realizing that we cannot do anything to earn our salvation. As the words of a famous hymn state:

> Nothing in my hands I bring,
> Simply to thy cross I cling...
>
> Not the labor of my hands
> Can fulfill thy law's demands....[1]

When did grace ever stop? "And if by grace, then it is no longer of works; otherwise grace is no longer grace. But if it is of works, it is no longer grace; otherwise work is no longer work" (Rom. 11:6). Paul reprimanded the Galatians for the same thing: "Did you receive the Spirit by the works of the law, or by the hearing of faith? Are ye so foolish? Having begun in the Spirit, are you now being made perfect by the flesh?" (Gal. 3:2-3).

God gets all the glory for our salvation. He will not share His glory with another. "I am the Lord, that is My name; and My glory I will not give to another, nor My praise to carved images" (Is. 42:8). God does choose to share His glory with his children (see Ps. 84:11; 2 Cor. 3:18), but any attempt to steal it ends in tragedy.

The Bible says, "[He] is able to keep you from stumbling, and to present you faultless before the presence of His glory with exceeding joy" (Jude 24). Presenting us faultless before the Father is Jesus' privilege. No one else, however spiritual, is able to do that — not your pastor, your best friend or your spouse. Do not let anyone else control your life. In the final count you are answerable only to Him.

Jesus died for you. You are owned by the Son of the living God; you are His property (Eph. 1:13-14) and sealed by His Spirit (Eph. 4:30). You are accountable to Him. His Spirit will guide, teach and instruct you in the truth. Someone else's revelation will be no excuse for your own failure.

Having a Submissive Spirit

Unfortunately, some leaders try to control and manipulate people under the guise of submission. Instead of encouraging them to hear and obey the voice of God, walk in the Spirit and nurture potential gifts, they have used and abused believers in order to build their own ministries or churches.

God is in the process of doing a giant rescue operation to bring out all those giftings, ministries and anointings that have lain dormant in the body of Christ. Gifts of healing and miracles are flowing through individual ministers, but much is buried within the church body. But it will come forth just as Lazarus came forth from the grave. God will bring forth the gifts He has deposited in your life if you believe in Him and seek His face.

A submissive spirit is openness to others, teachableness and an awareness that you could be wrong. Suppose you felt the

Holy Spirit told you to make a trip to Germany. Wouldn't you ask for prayer from people who loved you and could hear from the Lord? Perhaps a friend came to you saying, "I don't feel right in my spirit about your plans to go to Germany."

If you are submissive, you will be open to the possibility that you may be wrong. Seek the Lord sincerely with an open heart. The Lord may say, "You are to pray for Germany, but you are not to go there." Or He may say, "Proceed with your plans." You can ask for confirmation, but you must believe He is sending it.

When two people get married, the minister says, "Does any-one have any just cause or good reason why these two should not be joined together in holy matrimony?" He isn't asking for agreement or approval of the marriage. They have already made the decision and are going ahead unless there is a legitimate cause why they shouldn't (such as one still being legally married to another person). Just so, it's important that Christians are not controlled by the whims and prejudices of others.

---

[1]"Rock of Ages," by Augustus Montague Toplady (1740-1778).

TEN

FAITH — GOD'S VEHICLE

Wıthout faith it is impossible to please Him, for he who comes to God must believe that He is, and that He is a rewarder of those who diligently seek Him" (Heb. 11:6).

I know many people who worry because they feel they do not have enough faith. That is the problem — they *feel* they do not have enough faith. Faith — God's faith — has been imparted to us by the Spirit. It has nothing to do with how we feel. We believe with the heart, not the head. Jesus said to the Pharisees, "Why are you reasoning in your hearts?" (Luke 5:22).

When it comes to faith, we need to stay in the Spirit. Satan can make us feel depressed, down or discouraged, throwing thoughts of fear at us. What we feel is irrelevant; it's what we believe that will rule us.

The devil is a liar and a thief. When he comes around, say, "Satan, I know you're trying to discourage me, but what you've really done is remind me that I have received a word from the

Lord concerning this situation."

The Holy Spirit is an encourager. Discouragement and self-pity go against the very nature of the Holy Spirit.

Everything the Holy Spirit does bears fruit. It is impossible for Him to be barren. God is full of faith. He believes in Himself; He believes in the Son; He believes that the Holy Spirit can do wonders and great miracles in your life. God believes in His own ability and power, so we had better agree with Him. "Now to Him who is able to do exceedingly abundantly above all that we ask or [even] think, according to the power that works in us" (Eph. 3:20).

That promise is tied to the amount of God's power we allow to work in us. Even if we have broken the power of a negative religious spirit, it can come back in through a "works" mentality. The blessing of God is upon us in Christ Jesus. As we walk in Him, we will receive His provision by faith. There is no other way.

Faith is like electricity. Turn on the switch, and you have light. But without an electric current nothing will happen. Having the Word only in your mind produces no power; it merely gives you mental assent to the truth. Faith releases the power, but the Word of God (the switch) directs the flow and tells you what to believe.

Many things are not spelled out clearly in the Bible. We must seek the mind of the Spirit, which never contradicts the written Word. The Holy Spirit will tell us how to release our faith to believe for the blessing of God in our lives. If we seek first His kingdom and His righteousness, nothing will hinder our prayers. If other things come first in our lives, we open the door of interference to the devil and thereby step out of the flow of the Spirit.

It's like standing in the shower. The shower is spraying the water, but if we step out, we are getting out of the flow of water.

When the children of Israel came out of Egypt (see Num. 22 and 23), Balak, king of the Moabites, saw how many people there were and was frightened by them. He knew what they had done to the Amorites. He didn't want a battle, so he sent for the prophet Balaam. Balaam disobeyed God by going to Balak, who told him to curse the children of Israel. Balaam once again sought the Lord about it, although God had already told him three times that he was to bless the children of Israel. Although Balak was a great king, Balaam returned to Balak and said, "God is not a man, that He should lie, nor a son of man, that He should repent [or change His mind]. Has He said, and will He not do? Or has He spoken, and will He not make it good? Behold, I have received a command to bless; and He has blessed, and I cannot reverse it" (Num. 23:19-20).

We must tell Satan: "Satan, Christ has already blessed us, and you cannot prevent His blessing."

Satan's only power is to lie, and he will lie to you if you will listen. Reject his lies and speak the promises of God. Jesus said, "And you shall know the truth, and the truth shall make you free" (John 8:32). Free from what? Free from that which is true (in the natural). It is true that you may be in need, but the truth is that "my God shall supply all of your need according to his riches in glory by Christ Jesus" (Phil. 4:19). It is true that we are weak, but the truth is that "I can do all things through Christ who strengthens me" (Phil. 4:13). It may be true that I am sick, but the truth is "by His stripes we are healed" and "by whose stripes you were healed" (Is. 53:5; 1 Pet. 2:24). Satan uses many different lies to cause us to fear and to keep us from God's truth. If we learn to deal with the lie, then the fear will die.

Faith in His Promises

Before we were filled with the Holy Spirit, my husband and I prayed regularly for our parents' salvation. My mother was a sweet English lady who wouldn't harm a fly, but she did not know the Lord. My father had died when I was twelve. David's father was a nice Jewish man, and his mother was a devout Catholic full of good works. She revered God but didn't seem to have a personal relationship with Jesus. Although they sometimes visited our church and had heard the gospel message many times, they just didn't seem to get born again.

After being filled with the Holy Spirit, we started having meetings in our house. One weekend we took my mother to the church in South Chard. She was not at all used to meetings which lasted four hours or more. The worship and the praise, coupled with the presence of the Holy Spirit, stirred up something in her. She felt strange during those meetings. The choruses kept going around in her head, and she could not forget them. Though we had hoped she would be saved and filled with the Holy Spirit that weekend, it wasn't to happen without a trial of our faith.

We were hearing excited stories and testimonies about the South Chard Full Gospel Church. A deacon had been saved in a remarkable way. Although his wife had attended church regularly for about two years, he was apparently not interested.

One Sunday morning an evangelist taught on faith, exhorting the people to believe their prayers were answered at the time they prayed, according to Mark 11:24. She received her husband's salvation by faith. That night as her husband slept, she said to him, "Little do you know that you are saved!"

The next Sunday he decided to go to church with her, telling her that the only reason he was going was because he was tired of cooking Sunday dinner. During the worship he had an incredible vision of Jesus and began to weep. He experienced a mighty salvation, was baptized in the Holy Spirit and was unable to speak except to pray in tongues for two whole days. He began to devour his Bible and soon was ministering in the church meetings.

Hearing this increased our faith for our parents' salvation. As we prayed the Lord said to us, "Do you believe that salvation is for you and your house?" (see Acts 16:31). We said yes. He reminded us that "what things soever ye desire, when ye pray believe that ye receive them, and ye shall have them" (Mark 11:24, KJV).

Once more we claimed our family's salvation in faith, saying, "Lord, we will believe when we pray, not when we see." After we finished praying for each parent, we simply said, "Thank You, Lord. As far as we are concerned, they are saved; it is done. Their names are in Your book of life."

Every day we continued to thank Him. In our excitement we forgot that they didn't know Jesus yet, and we treated them as though they were already saved. For six weeks we continued to talk to my mom about Jesus until one day she suddenly went into a rage. She told us to leave her house and never return, saying that we had lost our minds.

Because this happened after we had received her salvation by faith, we gently said to her, "Jesus loves you." We thanked the Lord that she was saved, even though she didn't realize it yet. At times even the sound of my voice on the phone would anger her again. Putting down the phone, I'd say, "Thank You for her salvation!" Though my ears told me the opposite, I believed I had received her salvation by faith.

One Saturday evening Mother called me, this time sounding different. We chatted for a while, but I was expecting her to explode at any minute. Then she said, "I'm not sure what to do tomorrow — I'm bored." I suggested watching a movie on television, but she was tired of television. Then I suggested she visit her sister, but she didn't want to do that either. Finally she said, "I thought I might come to your meeting."

Hesitating, I said, "You will find it noisy and a little strange. I don't really know if you would like it."

"Don't tell me what I would or wouldn't like. How do you know?" she retorted.

"All right," I said. "You are more than welcome."

She came, hungry for the Lord, and got saved, filled with the Spirit and baptized in water. Because of our faith, something happened in the realm of the spirit. Satan can't stand against faith. He has to bow to Jesus.

The salvation of David's father came next. Although he was Jewish, he did not practice his religion. A mild, easygoing man, he wasn't against David's conversion ten years prior; he just wasn't interested for himself.

After we were filled with the Spirit and received his salvation by faith, things began to happen. For several weeks there was no change, but we kept thanking Jesus that he was saved.

David's mother related to us how he finally met Jesus. In the middle of the night he suddenly sat up in bed. She turned on the light to see what was wrong. Putting his hands in the air, he said, while still asleep, "Jesus, my Messiah."

When he awoke the next morning he was changed. A few weeks later, he responded to an altar call at a Morris Cerullo crusade in London, going forward to confirm with his mind what had already happened in his heart. A short time later David's mother raised her hand for salvation at a local meeting in our hometown.

These experiences gave us faith to believe for others. When we ministered in schools, we received salvation in faith for the youth. At first fifty or so would be saved, but soon we were believing the Lord for hundreds. As we exercised our faith, we saw great outpourings of the Spirit.

Within a year our house meeting had moved into the local town hall to accommodate all of the people attending. Teenagers were awestruck as the Lord revealed the secrets of their hearts. Revival was breaking out in the local schools.

God had seen the hunger in our hearts for His supernatural work. We were willing to pay whatever price was necessary to see His power become effective in our lives and ministry. In times of revival expect radical things to happen!

ELEVEN

DIVINE VISITATIONS

I love this scripture: "Thou hast granted me life and favor, and thy visitation hath preserved my spirit" (Job 10:12, KJV). Glory to God! His visitations are real and powerful. Believe for them; expect them.

I have experienced many different kinds of visitations. Sometimes the perfume of the Lord will come upon people in a meeting, usually resulting in deliverance. The smell varies; at times it smells like lilies, and at other times like roses or sweet apples. At one meeting the smell of freshly baked bread filled the room (and there were no bakeries nearby). At other times people have felt oil on their heads or hands. In a large communion service with Morris Cerullo in London years ago, the auditorium was filled with a very light rain, which I felt on my face and hands for nearly an hour.

Other visitations last longer. Their specific purpose is to bring a revelation of Jesus and the Father. You cannot choose to have a visitation. But if you believe in the realm of the supernatural, visitations will come from time to time. These usually are personal, although they can be shared to encourage and minister to others. The Holy Spirit does not reveal anything that is contrary to Scripture, but He enlightens our eyes to understand spiritual realities.

While we were living in Orlando in 1986, one visitation lasted for seven days. During this time the Holy Spirit arranged circumstances to make it possible for Him to come and do what He had planned. David was helping a friend start a business, and he left the house every day at 8:00 A.M., returning around 5:30 P.M. My two children attended a local Christian school, leaving home at 8:00 A.M. and returning at 3:30 P.M. Each day as I sat waiting on the Lord, the Holy Spirit would come upon me at 9:00 A.M., lifting me into the heavenlies and showing me many things. Each day He showed me awesome things pertaining to Jesus' desire for His bride. It was wonderful, and I had such an intimate time with the Lord.

Knowing that Jesus loves us is one thing; experiencing it is an entirely different thing. I felt His love so much that I could hardly talk about it. Each day at 3:00 P.M. the anointing lifted, and I was back in my home in time to get supper and see to the needs of my children.

In Virginia in 1992 I had a similar visitation that lasted three and a half weeks. This was not confined to home, but it happened often while I was driving. As before, the Spirit lifted me up into the heavenlies, although I could often still hear the music from my car. I would find myself with Jesus and the angels, arriving at my destination with no recollection of how I got there. Day after day this continued.

One day in particular I saw Jesus with a young girl. It looked like me. I felt as if I represented the body of Christ as His betrothed. I saw the relationship develop between Jesus and the young girl. He was wonderful — full of grace, kindness and love — and she fell in love with Him. As she spent time in His presence, she became just like Him. God's Word tells us, "But we all, with unveiled face, beholding as in a mirror the glory of the Lord, are being transformed into the same image from glory to glory, just as by the Spirit of the Lord" (2 Cor. 3:18). That is exactly what happened. She manifested the same grace and kindness. Their love for each other was an awesome thing to see.

Finally ready, she became His bride. I saw the wedding feast and her ruling and reigning with Him. People from every race, tribe and nation came to worship Him before His throne.

When I am praying for people and see rejection, pain, anxiety, worry and fear on their faces, I tell them, "I want you to know how much Jesus loves you — how much He absolutely adores His bride. I have seen His face when he looks at us as though our relationship with Him is the most wonderful thing that has ever happened." The Song of Solomon is not just an allegory; it is a love story. We are His love, the object of all of His affections.

Angels

Angels were a normal part of the life of the New Testament church. Two angels spoke to the disciples when Jesus was taken up into heaven (Acts 1). The angel of the Lord opened the prison doors for the apostles (Acts 5). Another angel appeared to Philip and told him to go to Gaza (Acts 8). An angel spoke to Cornelius about sending his servants to Joppa to get Simon (Acts 10). An angel loosed Peter from his cell in prison (Acts 12). When Paul and Silas were imprisoned, an earthquake shook the prison. It must have been a band of angels that unlocked the doors and loosed their fetters (Acts 16). The angel of the Lord smote Herod (Acts 12). Angels ministered to Jesus on many occasions. Many instances of angels ministering to God's people are recorded throughout the Bible.

Though we aren't really conscious of their presence, angels are always around ministering to us. But we can only see spiritual things with the eyes of faith. If you don't believe there are angelic ministers in your life, you will never see them. You cannot see the things of the spirit if you have unbelief. Angels are a part of my walk with God. At times someone will say,

"You must not worship angels." I don't worship them; in fact, the only angels who would allow themselves to be worshipped are demonic angels, or demons. They love to be worshipped.

Religious demons try to seduce us to idolize personalities, forms, programs, buildings, great ministries, our church or even our pastor. But only God is worthy of worship. "That no flesh should glory in His presence....He who glories, let him glory in the Lord" (1 Cor. 1:29,31). We should be grateful for God's gifts of various ministries, but we are not allowed to place them above the Lord in our affections.

While in Columbus, Ohio, a few years ago, I went out for a walk. An angel walked with me, telling me about the neighborhood for which my friends had been praying. He told me about the little church on the corner. He showed me the homes of some people who would be leaving the area and others where new families would be moving in. When I returned to Columbus the next year, many of these changes had taken place.

There is an angel who helps me write, and he tells me things that help me to pray properly for people's needs. Sometimes he sits with me while I drive and tells me things about Jesus.

When my daughter Faith was in fifth grade, she liked to wake up in the mornings to the music of Amy Grant. The volume had to be just right or she would go back to sleep. One morning the music was too soft, and she drifted back to sleep. Suddenly the volume turned up long enough to awaken her and then turned down again.

The next day she awoke early and played her tape through one side. Since it was still early, she stayed in her bed. The tape stopped playing, ejected, was turned over and began to play on the other side.

Thirty minutes later, a friend who was staying in our home came out of the bedroom. Her face shone as she said, "I was quietly laying in bed praising God, and the door opened. I didn't see anyone come in, but suddenly the whole room filled with the scent of a beautiful perfume." Her room, next to Faith's, had apparently been visited by the same angel.

At one time we lived in Newberry, Florida, on a farm with a

pool. We always prayed that an angel would look after any child in our pool. While several children swam one afternoon, each child saw the same angel standing in the same place at the same time. Apparently he let them see him so they would know that they were divinely protected.

In 1991 we were staying in a friend's apartment in St. Petersburg, Florida. I had been praying for signs and wonders so that the nations would know the awesomeness of God. One evening while the others went to a movie, I stayed in my room. As I lay across the bed asking God to pour out His Spirit, I saw a light out of the corner of my eye. Looking around, I saw a figure standing near the doorway of the room, dressed in a fine white silk robe and holding a piece of white material folded over his right arm. The seven-foot-tall, slender figure stood gazing at me, his eyes full of light. A thought came to me that he was black and not just dark. I had never seen a black angel before.

"Who are you?" I asked.

He spelled out loud, "J-A-L-A."

"That's a funny name," I replied.

He answered, "You couldn't say my name." I thought that his name was probably too long to pronounce.

I didn't talk with him further but went into the living room to wait for my friend and my two daughters to return. When they got home, I did not say anything to them about the man in the other room.

My daughter Faith said good night and went straight to bed. She is the kind of person who falls asleep as soon as her head touches the pillow, and she sleeps soundly. After thirty minutes she started calling loudly, "Mama! Mama!"

I ran to her room and found her sitting up in her bed, her eyes wide open. "Did you call me, Mama?" she asked.

I told her no, but she pressed me. "Are you sure you didn't come in and call my name?"

"No, I really didn't," I told her.

"But, Mama, didn't you call my name in a deep man's voice?" she asked.

"No, Faith, I didn't."

"Who was it then?" she asked

I told her about the angel who spoke to me and said it must have been he calling her name. Breathing a sigh of relief she slipped back under the sheet and fell sound asleep.

As I went to bed that night I was still aware of the presence of the angel, but we did not talk. When I awoke the next morning, he was still standing near the door. There was nothing at all frightening about his presence; it was awesome, yet gentle. I was puzzled. He had a round, white hat on his head and looked like someone from one of the African nations. I felt I needed to get some confirmation about this experience.

I called a prophetic friend of mine and simply said, "Hi, how are you?"

After talking for a couple of minutes, Bob asked me what the Lord was showing me. Hesitating, I said, "Well, I was praying, and I saw a man...."

That's as far as I got because he interrupted me. "He's tall and slender, and he's wearing a long white silk robe with some of it folded over his right arm, isn't he?" I just about fell off the chair.

Bob continued, "He's black and not just dark, isn't he?" He had said the exact same words I had thought when I first saw the angel: He's black and not just dark. When Bob said those words, a peace came into my heart. Then the angel smiled and just disappeared.

"He is the angel over one of the African nations," Bob continued. "He has come to call you to that nation."

But I didn't even speak to him, I thought. How gracious he was to have stayed for twenty-four hours, waiting until I had the peace of God.

"Which nation was he from?" asked Bob.

"I didn't ask him," I sighed, feeling foolish.

"Well, now you'll have to pray and ask God to show you where he was from, because you are going to have to make a response." Bob then ended the conversation with "I'll pray for you."

I asked the Lord to forgive me and to make it clear to me

what nation He wanted me to go to.

The following morning when I awoke, there stood in the same place another angel, short and slight but very pleasant to look at. He also wore a white robe, but it was more like a gown with gold edging. On his head was a small, round, flat hat, slightly different from that of the first angel. His features were fine, and he was also black. He spoke just one sentence: "Will you come?"

I knew he was talking about Nigeria. Without hesitating, I said yes.

Later, as I sat drinking a cup of coffee in the living room, he suddenly appeared before the small coffee table which was in front of me. "Are you sure that you will come?" he asked.

I was surprised, but again I said yes.

I thought about Nigeria all day, asking the Lord for some other confirmation. That night as I washed a few dishes, the angel appeared again in the doorway. "Are you really sure that you will come?" he asked again.

"Yes," I replied very firmly. I felt a little irritated. It seemed as if he didn't believe me when I said I would go.

I asked the Father, "Why did he ask me that repeatedly?"

Immediately God said, "Many people have said they would go, but because there was no money in it, they never went."

The Lord's words pierced my heart. "Give us the right contacts then, Lord," I said.

God is now putting it all together. Our ministry receives a lot of requests for books from Nigerian pastors, schools and individuals. We always send something because of my promise to that nation.

About a year before this episode, while walking on a beach in Virginia, the Spirit of God fell on me, and I could not move another step. The presence of the Lord was in front of me like a pillar of light. He spoke to me saying, "Both of you will minister to thousands of black children. You will have meetings with twenty to thirty thousand children at a time, with awesome signs, wonders and miracles that you have never seen before. I will pour out a great revival upon these children."

Although I have told few people about these experiences, we have had several letters from pastors in Nigeria telling me that they knew I had angelic visitations concerning their nation. We received a prophecy from John Watson's church in Marion, Ohio, that we would have meetings with twenty to thirty thousand black children at a time, with more signs, wonders and miracles than we had imagined. They knew nothing of the Lord's word to me personally or of those angelic visitors.

Angels can take many forms. Paul saw a man of Macedonia in a vision: "And a vision appeared to Paul in the night. A man of Macedonia stood and pleaded with him, saying, 'Come over to Macedonia and help us' " (Acts 16:9).

The angel of the Lord led Peter out of prison. Peter then ran to Mary's house and knocked at the door, and a young lady named Rhoda answered. She did not open the door, but she told the others that Peter was there. They told her that she was mad, but she insisted that Peter was at the door. "It is his angel," they said (Acts 12:13-16). The early church was used to angels looking like people. We are told to be hospitable, "for...some have unwittingly entertained angels" (Heb. 13:2). An angel must look similar to a human if it is possible for us to entertain them unaware.

Two angels met Lot at Sodom (Gen. 19), and he took them to his house for the night. "Then he made them a feast, and baked unleavened bread, and they ate" (Gen. 19:3). Shortly after that, some men from the city came to Lot's house, demanding that Lot deliver the two visitors into their hands. Obviously the two angels were visiting the city in the form of men and looked like everyone else.

Over the last few years there has been a tremendous move of God in the jungle areas of Borneo and on the islands of Sarawak. Many tribes have been saved. God has manifested His supernatural power to these desolate tribes in many different ways. Pictures and words depicting the gospel story have appeared in the sky. Miracles and visitations have occurred even to the children.

During a recent visit there, a Malaysian friend of ours named

Chris Choo learned that it was very common for angels to appear to the tribal peoples. Surprised by his question, "What do angels look like?" they replied simply, "They look just like us, of course." Angelic visitations are normal events to these tribal people.

On my first visit to Israel, as I visited all the usual historic places, an angel accompanied me, often touching my arm and whispering with a laugh, "He isn't here." Scripture says that "God looks on His enemies and laughs" (see Ps. 2:4; Ps. 37:13; Ps. 59:8). As I stood inside the garden tomb, my last stop, the angel touched my arm again. "He certainly isn't here," he laughed triumphantly. It was so loud to me that I was sure everyone had heard it. But as I went out the little doorway, I laughed too. I am sure some people thought I was rather irreverent.

On my second visit an angel dressed in the uniform of an Israeli army soldier appeared to my friend and me as we visited Abraham and Sarah's tomb. He answered Doreen's questions about a festival to take place, said good-bye and vanished completely within seconds. The presence of God was so overwhelming that we could not stand up for nearly an hour.

Later, a man with a look of fear on his face stopped to ask us a question. As I stood to answer him, his whole countenance changed in front of my eyes. The anointing of God, still so strong from our conversation with the angel, caused the spirit of fear to leave him. The Lord revealed to me that as we minister with His anointing, all we will have to do is speak His words, and the people of Israel, as well as others, will receive deliverance.

TWELVE

INTERCESSION

God uses us in different kinds of intercession and prayer. Jesus spoke of the prayer of faith: "Therefore I say to you, whatever things you ask when you pray, believe that you receive them, and you will have them" (Mark 11:24). I translate this verse like this: "When you pray, believe you have it, and then you will get it." Jesus spoke of the woman who went to the unjust judge and kept knocking at his door until he granted her request for justice (Luke 18:2-6). There is a time to keep on knocking, but then there is a time to receive the answer by faith.

Our prayers must be initiated by the Holy Spirit, who will reveal the mind of the Father to us. I spent many hours praying according to my own mind before being filled with the Spirit. I had no idea what was on God's heart or how to find out. But God very graciously blessed my willingness and had grace for my ignorance.

Our children were only concerned with their immediate surroundings when they were small. But as they grew, they discovered the interests and concerns that David and I shared, and they understood some of our long-term plans. Eventually they understood how they fit into our lives and what part they had to play. They became a part of the action, sharing our desire and commitment to minister to the children of the nations. They understood our destiny.

God wants us to know His heart. As we grow in Him, the Holy Spirit will show us the part we have in His great purposes for our own family, for His church and for the nations.

Christians who have not been drinking from the well of living water can have dry spirits. They may not have experienced a refilling of the Spirit for several years. Christians are meant to experience the presence of the Lord and His Spirit continually. There is one baptism but many fillings. The book of Acts gives the example of the disciples: "And they were all filled with the Holy Spirit" (Acts 2:4). Two chapters later, we read, "They were all filled with the Holy Spirit..." (Acts 4:31). Obviously they needed more than just one filling. Religious spirits do not mind if you know about the presence of God in your mind, as long as it doesn't affect your life. They do not want you to experience fresh fillings from the Holy Spirit.

Waiting on the Lord for the Holy Spirit to reveal the Father's will is a part of all intercession.

> Likewise the Spirit also helps in our weaknesses. For we do not know what we should pray for as we ought, but the Spirit Himself makes intercession for us with groanings which cannot be uttered. Now He who searches the hearts knows what the mind of the Spirit is, because He makes intercession for the saints according to the will of God (Rom. 8:26-27).

Children can also be strong intercessors, weeping for others with awesome visions and prophetic words as they pray. It is not enough for your children and teens to be good kids; teach them how to be anointed, godly young people who hear from God.

There is a big difference between just being good and being godly.

During the Gulf War we prayed regularly for our troops. One evening a neighbor and I and her two children, along with my daughters, Faith and Lisa, gathered around the fireplace to pray. My daughter Faith had a "mini-movie vision" which she described as follows: "I see an American plane which has been hit, and it is coming down. The pilot is OK. He is walking in the desert, looking for somewhere to hide, because enemy soldiers are quite near. We need to pray for him to find a hiding place." She stopped and prayed. "I see an American plane looking for him, but he is too far in the desert for them to come. We need to pray that they will travel further and find him."

We prayed that the rescue plane would not turn back until they found the pilot. Later, we read the whole story of the rescue in the July 1992 issue of *Reader's Digest*. It even related the part about the rescue plane nearly turning back because they were running short of fuel.

God will share His secrets with those who intercede for His kingdom. The Scriptures say, "Eye has not seen, nor ear heard, nor have entered into the heart of man the things which God has prepared for those who love Him. But God has revealed them to us, through His Spirit. For the Spirit searches all things, yes, the deep things of God" (1 Cor. 2:9-10). In Deuteronomy 29:29 we read, "The secret things belong to the Lord our God, but those things which are revealed belong to us and to our children forever." Expect God to share things with you.

The Lord may reveal something to you that isn't even in your prayers. One day I sensed the presence of an angel. In a vision I saw a ram with large, curled horns standing in the heavens. I knew that it was a demonic principality. As I watched, I saw an angel come from the corner of heaven with a large sword in his hand. The angel cut off the head of the ram, but the body of the ram kept standing for a little while before it collapsed.

I asked the Holy Spirit what it meant, and He said, "This day President Amin of Uganda and his government are fallen in the spirit."

At times God will give your spirit a revelation, but you may not see the natural manifestation until later. Idi Amin's government actually came to a natural end about seven months later, but in the spiritual realm God had ended it that day.

While attending a prayer meeting in Orlando several years ago, the Lord told me to go into the next room by myself. Not wanting to disturb anyone, I went quietly into the room. As I stood there, a bright light came down and engulfed me. I sank to the floor and felt my spirit rising toward the light.

The next moment I sensed that I was in Jerusalem, standing inside the mosque of Omar, observing rows of men kneeling down on mats and praying. My first thought was to get out of there quickly. But then I saw Jesus walk past the men and touch several of them on the shoulder. He walked back toward me and said: "The men I have touched are going to be saved. I am sending my servants to minister to them and tell them the gospel story."

Then we left the mosque and walked down a street in the old part of Jerusalem. Jesus pointed out several people. There was an elderly couple selling bread from a cart. He told me their business was not doing very well, but their friends and neighbors were going to help them. As He pointed out a very attractive dark-haired Jewish girl of about twenty, He said, "Her fiancé is seeking for the truth. I am sending someone to witness to him so he will be saved." He continued with another couple. When we got to the end of the street, the Lord turned to me and said, "You have to go now."

"Oh, no," I responded, "I'll just stay here with You."

Jesus said again, "You have to go now. I am going to visit the prayer meeting at the convent." Suddenly I was back in the room in Orlando, unable to move from the floor for some time.

At another time, as David prayed for some teenagers, I stood behind them. The Holy Spirit came upon these teenagers, and I felt myself falling back toward the floor. Surrounded by a light, I saw Jesus standing in a gold chariot above me. He reached out His hand and pulled me up into the chariot next to Him.

The chariot began to go faster and higher. I had a sensation of tremendous speed. I caught a glimpse of an ocean beneath me, then a Mideastern city with white buildings. Above this city sat a cross-legged, arrogant-looking spirit dressed in Eastern clothes.

I asked Jesus if He was going to do anything about that spirit. He said, "No, not now." A moment later I stood in a wheat field outside a town in South Africa. David was by my side, and Jesus was standing on a small hill a little farther away. Several black children came out of the tall wheat, and David preached the gospel and pointed them toward Jesus. They walked toward Him without averting their gaze. They didn't appear to notice my presence as they passed me.

More children came out of the wheat field, and the same thing happened again. Very soon hundreds of these beautiful black children were streaming out of the field, walking to the little hill where Jesus stood without taking their eyes from Him. Finally there were so many that it wasn't necessary to preach. A mighty move of the Spirit took place. Jesus came and put His arms around David and me.

Suddenly I was back in my room, unable to move for nearly fifteen minutes.

Satan wants us to fear strong anointings like this, because he knows that fear will stop us from yielding to the Holy Spirit. But Jesus said, "What man is there among you who, if his son asks for bread, will give him a stone? Or if he asks for a fish, will he give him a serpent?" (Matt. 7:9-10).

Many people who are praying for revival do not know what they are praying for. When revival comes, many supernatural things happen that are strange to the religious or skeptical mind. At times God waits until His people are desperately hungry so they won't dismiss the food He offers to them.

A few years ago as we ministered in Michigan, the Holy Spirit began to move in a powerful way. Some people laughed, others wept, others were delivered, and still others were praising with their arms raised. The Lord ministered in many individual ways, and though it looked chaotic, God was in control.

I noticed the pastor standing alone in a corner, and asked him if he was all right.

"I have lost control of this, and I don't know what to do." he replied.

"Have you been praying for revival?" I asked.

His answer was an emphatic yes.

Then the Holy Spirit told me what to say to him. "God is giving you a little taste of revival in order for you to realize what you have been praying for. Often in revival, God takes over, doing what He wants. We have to keep out of His way and follow the Holy Spirit, so don't be afraid."

He smiled and visibly relaxed. Although the New Testament says, "Let all things be done decently and in order" (1 Cor. 14:40), we must realize that God's idea of "decently and in order" may be vastly different from ours.

My heart's desire is that this book has created a desire in you to believe for an intimate relationship with the Holy Spirit. Desire to know Him so well that His supernatural ways will be evident in your personal life and in your church services, so that you will glorify your Savior, the Lord Jesus Christ.

Parenting by the Sprit
by Kathie Walters

The Spirit of False Judgement
by Kathie Walters

The Visitation
by Kathie & Faith Walters

Kids in Combat
by David Walters

Equipping the Younger Saints
By David Walters

Children Aflame
By David Walters

Bull in a China Shop
by Gary Folds

CHILDREN'S BIBLE STUDY BOOKS
Ages 7-14
The Armor of God
(illustrated). By David Walters

Fact or Fantasy
(illustrated) By David Walters

Being a Christian
(illustrated) By David Walters

Fruit of the Spirit
(illustrated) by David Walters

For a catalogue
and current pricing:

Good News Fellowship Ministries
220 Sleepy Creek Road
Macon, GA 31210
Phone:(912)757-8071   Fax:**(912)757-0136**